Smile America

Chris and Daya Devi-Doolin

Padaran Publications

Deltona, FL 32725

Smile America, by Chris and Daya Devi-Doolin. Copyright © 2010, Padaran Publications, Deltona, FL 32725.

All rights reserved. Excerpts from *Returning to the Source*, Copyright 2001 and excerpts from *Super Vita-Minds: How to Stop Saying I Hate You...To Yourself*, Copyright © 2000, Padaran Publications, Deltona, FL 32725.

The First Edition of **A Course in Miracles** is now free from copyright. We are quoting from the First Edition. Permission was granted from the Authors of *Born A Healer*, Chunyi Lin and Gary Rebstock of Spring Forest Publishing, **www.springforestqigong.com** to use excerpt.

ISBN 978-1-87794518-2
ISBN 1-877945-18-8
Library of Congress Card Catalog Number 2009909192
First Edition
1 2 3 4 5 6 7 8 9 10

Padaran Publications
Sales www.padaran.com
Email padaran@padaran.com
Telephone (386) 532-5308
Graphic Designer: Cheron Boyd of Nine Ocean Media
Illustrations: Daya Devi-Doolin

Printed in the U.S.A.
Padaran Publications
(386) 532-5308
1794 N. Acadian Drive
Deltona, FL 32725

Chris and Daya Devi-Doolin   Smile America

Books Written by Daya Devi-Doolin

The Only Way Out Is In: The Secrets of the 14 Realms to Love, Happiness and Success!
Super Vita-Minds: How To Stop Saying I Hate You…To Yourself
Americans Saving Ourselves Together: How to Thrive in the 21st Century
Dabney's Handbook on A Course in Miracles
All I Need to Know….Is Inside (A Pocket Bite Book with cartoons)
Dabney, Dormck & Wiggles' Slakaduman Adventures
Dormck and the Temple of the Healing Light
Sikado's Star of Aragon (Dabney & Dormck Adventures)

Books Written by Chris & Daya Devi-Doolin

Smile America
Hidden Manna: How You Can Interpret Your Dreams
Returning to The Source

Smile America

Chris and Daya Devi-Doolin

Chris and Daya Devi-Doolin   Smile America

Table of Contents

Acknowledgements		i
Preface	Daya Devi-Doolin	iii
Quote	Chunyi Lin and &	
	Gary Rebstock Co-Authors	
	of *Born A Healer*	
Foreword	Inez Bracy	viii
Introduction	Cee Cee Sneed	xi
The Inspiration for our music		xii

A Healing Connection	1
Magical Encounter	2
New Opportunities	3
What Does Level Seven Mean?	5

Chris' Brief Musical Bio	5
Self-Imposed Cocoon	6
An Electric Guitar Pilfered	8
Gangsters and Gashes	10
Click Fast Forward	11
One Chance to Be Chosen for Folk City	11
We Can See Restored Prosperity	13
Metaphysics and MIDI	14
A Synchronistic Meeting	15
Daya's Journey	16
Why I Learned the Guitar	17
"Pack Your Belongings and Leave Your Security Behind"	18

The Trek to Homelessness	20
Our Romantic Synergistic Meeting to Now!	21
Where Do We Sleep?	23
Hidden Resources	24
The Genesis of Smile America	25
Tour Map of Our Musical Journey	28
Music Events	30
Humorous (in retrospect) Happenings	32
Move into your SMILING phase America	36
Spiritual Guidance	39
Lyrics to Our Smile America CD	41
Returning to the Source Part 1	60
Returning to the Source Part 2	
Excerpt from *Super Vita-Minds: How to Stop Saying I Hate You…To Yourself!*	
Appendix: Excerpts from three of Daya Devi-Doolin's books	91

Acknowledgments

When we were homeless street musicians, we woke up every day giving thanks to the Creator for helping us be successful that day. We still today want to give thanks and acknowledge God as the Source of everything in our lives. Like branches grow from the trunk which grows from the roots of a tree, many have helped us along the way. We give thanks to everyone, family, friends and acquaintances that have touched our lives and supported us on our journey. Our parents brought the gift of music into our lives.

Life's experiences have been the source of our lyrics and music since finding each other through God's Grace.

Chris and Daya Devi-Doolin Smile America

Preface

When Chris and I lived in the Boston area, we played music at many venues including concerts, coffeehouses, colleges and festivals. One of the memorable times was when were played at the John Hancock Auditorium for the Boston's 2nd Annual Awards Show.

Though we didn't know it at the time, we stood backstage with many celebrities in the making back then waiting our turn to go onstage. We were the act before Gloria Gaynor. Maurice Starr was one of the guest performers that night. We never met him or the other artists personally, but all our names were on a program that I kept for our scrapbook.

When you read the foreword of our book, you will find out that Inez Bracy was the focal point in our meeting Maurice Starr nearly thirty years after and a thousand miles away from the Awards Show in Boston. After I met Maurice with Inez, I went home and looked in our scrapbook for that year and found the program that listed us, known as Abraham's Seed back then, and saw Maurice's name on the program as well.

I took the program back to him the next time we had our first recording session with him. We were amazed and could not get over it. He said, "Yes, that's me and the groups I was introducing at the time." We were all amazed that here we were now in the present, together and getting to work with each other on this exciting music project we call Smile America.

Knowing what I know about the Universe and Universal Mind, once you send a thought in motion with feeling, belief, intention and expectation, it will manifest for you. In will include all the details and more to enhance your world. I have always known and shared with Chris that God was preparing other people as well as preparing us for the time and day we would meet. We both had to be ready for whomever that might be to work together in harmony, integrity, trust and professionalism. Two of those people I am referring to are Maurice Starr and Inez Bracy. I was destined to meet Inez and I felt it so strongly to attend her talk and book signing in spring of 2009.

Little did I know that she knew and was friends with Maurice. So we met as you will soon find out and it still brings tears to my eyes when I get into the feeling that God has provided a way for us to share in this venture of a book, recording, and DVD of our musical life. *Smile America* is our call to be lifted up just as we have experienced being miraculously guided so many times.

Maurice is the one who suggested that this book be written in conjunction with our CD. He has produced the DVD and video-graphed it for us. We are truly grateful for all he has done to help put this project together and for just being in the *Presence* at all times in working with us. We are thankful that his and Inez's paths intertwined with ours in such a marvelous way.

As host of my radio show called (after the title of my book) *The Only Way Out Is In*, I have the opportunity to meet many wonderful, talented and loving people who are experts in their field. Their joy is in helping others to find a higher level of joy, love and peace in their lives. They only want for others to be healthy, successful and happy.

One of the authors I met is a Certified Master of Qigong. I was made aware of him about a year ago having received a mini CD of Spring Forest Qigong out of the blue from him. I did the standing exercises that are demonstrated on his CD gift. It was wonderful to practice these exercises. I could feel the energy.

One year later, I was contacted and asked by his publicist if I would like to interview this author and Master of Qigong on my radio show. As most publicists will send me a copy of the author's work so I can review their message before our interview, she sent me his book, *Born A Healer*. I found out he had a Co-Author, Gary Rebstock, who was taught by Chunyi Lin and has been certified as a Spring Forest Qigong Teacher.

Upon seeing his photo again, reading their book and listening to the CD that was sent along, I found it was the same man I had heard from a year ago. So we were destined to meet at this time. Upon reading their book, non-stop after receiving it in the mail, I came to page 101 and stopped in my tracks. It was suggested to me by Spirit and apparent that I was to ask permission to quote them for our book, *Smile America*. That section is below.

"Chinese scholars, in their long time observation, learned that over-excitement affects the heart energy, anger affects the liver energy, fear affects the kidney energy, depression affects the lung energy and too much mental work makes imbalances in the stomach and pancreas energy. If we let these powerful, "negative" emotions stay in the body for too long, the vibration of these feelings will certainly cause blockages, make damage to the organs, and we get sick.

Think of your own life. You respond much differently to a smile than you do to an angry look. A smile is uplifting. It makes you feel better. A smile helps your body relax. Your respiration, heart rate, immune system, every part of you is positively affected. An angry look creates the opposite reaction.

We like the energy vibration from a smile but we don't like the energy vibration from an angry look. The angry vibration hurts the liver energy in your body, while the vibration from a smile will comfort your soul and helps the body to heal.

Every day in big and little ways we have the opportunity to choose "heaven or hell." We have stress, anger, fear, jealousy, because we choose to have them. They cause energy blockages and damage to the body.

We have many choices. We can choose to ignore these "negative" things when they happen. We can choose to forget them, forgive them, or we can choose to accept them in a positive way. For instance, we can choose to think they are great opportunities to help us grow. And, in reality, that's exactly what they are – great opportunities for us to grow and to purify our own energy.

We have love, kindness, forgiveness and happiness because we choose to have them. They help to heal the body, mind and spirit. The vibration of love energy is the most powerful in healing, whether healing yourself or helping others.

These are not only the most positive choices; they are also the most practical ones. They help you and heal you, while the others hurt you.

I think the choice is an easy one. Practicing Spring Forest Qigong can help lead you to that healthy choice every day. Try it and you'll see. You'll soon find yourself making that healthy choice more and more without even thinking about it.

We are so quick to judge things. Something that seems very negative can turn out to be very positive."

Chunyi Lin and Gary Rebstock, Authors of #1 Best-Selling book, *Born A Healer*. *Website is www.bornahealer.com or www.springforestqigong.com.*

Foreword

The background story of how I was asked to write this foreword to *Smile America* is an interesting story that began three years ago when I knew very little about Daya Devi-Doolin, except that I wanted to meet her. As a Lifestyle Transitions Coach, author and motivational speaker, I conduct personal development workshops.

At one of my workshops in 2006 a participant, Marcie said "Inez you should meet my friend Daya, in fact she has written a book and I will bring it to you tomorrow." The next day she brought me the book *Super Vita Minds: How to Stop Saying I Hate You...To Yourself.* I was intrigued with the title and opened the book to discover a jewel of information that was totally understandable and useful.

I called Daya and we spoke briefly but never met. Now fast-forward three years. I was doing a book signing with another author, Dr. Nalani Valentine, at the local African American Museum. At the end of our talk, this very unassuming lady walked up to me and said, "Hi, I'm Daya Devi-Doolin and I was inspired to come here today to meet you." Imagine my surprise! I said "Fantabulous! I've been waiting to meet you for three years!" This started what has become a tremendous friendship and I'm delighted to have her in my life.

Daya as the thought leader invited me to be an author in the book *Americans Saving Ourselves Together* and I immediately said yes. This book is the genesis for *Smile

America. The first time I heard Daya and her husband Chris play *Smile America* my friends and I told them "this has got to get out to the masses." We didn't know how this would happen but.... Daya totally believes in God providing an answer and one was provided.

I invited Daya to be a guest with me on a weekly TV show to talk about *Americans Saving Ourselves Together* and she agreed. While we were in the car, out of nowhere I said, "I'm going to call Maurice because I'd like for him to hear *Smile America*." Daya gave me this incredulous look and said, "Do you mean Maurice Starr the Promoter?" I said yes, he is a friend and I called him. He was interested so we scheduled a meeting for Daya and Maurice to meet.

Maurice and I have been friends for a few years but I have never talked to him about nor introduced him to any artist. I've always felt and wanted to keep my friendship with Maurice free of 'business.' I witnessed a miracle the night Daya and Maurice met. Maurice was very gregarious, gracious and I could see he was thrilled with the music. He started giving ideas and suggestions almost immediately.

Reading *Smile America* you will discover many messages. Some of the messages will speak directly to you and others will cause you to ponder. The strongest message is that smiles and sadness cannot live in the same place.

Many have experienced pain and unhappiness over the last couple of years because of the downturn in the economy. Daya and Chris believe as I do that outside circumstances (economy) are like a thermometer, stocks go up and everybody is happy (whether you have stocks or not), stocks go down and everybody is sad.

We believe that it's up to us to be the thermostat by realizing we carry our economy inside and hold our temperature steady. Being a thermostat means that by having faith in ourselves, in our Father and standing on the promises of God, we hold steady.

Smile America is not about having a Pollyanna attitude nor is it about wearing 'rose colored' glasses.

Reading this book is about looking deeply into yourself to access your knowledge, your divinity and know that you can and will thrive. You can thrive in any economy because you carry your economy (God) inside. So read on and start improving your life today.

~Inez Bracy, MS, Lifestyle Transitions Coach, TV Guest and Radio Host, Author Rejuvenate Your Life in 21 Days, Co-Author & Recipient of NABE Pinnacle Book Achievement Award for Americans Saving Ourselves Together: How to Thrive in the 21st Century

Introduction

Sometimes our joy is the source of our smile, yet other times it's our smile that is the source of our joy. Smiling not only brightens our face and lightens our burdens, but also lightens those burdens of people around us.

Smiling is the outward expression of an inward feeling. Have you ever noticed that you cannot smile and be angry at the same time? The more you smile, the more you infect others–that is, in a positive, uplifting way! Smiling is free, enhances your beauty, and instantly puts people at ease.

Being joyful makes us smile but you must also realize that sometimes it's the smile that brings about our joyfulness---think about that! Either way, it chases away your blues and those of others by putting on a happy face and flashing your pearly whites as much as possible today. You'll instantly give both your mood and appearance a boost! You cannot be unaffected by someone approaching you with a big, broad smile! It's infectious, contagious, and an easy way to instantly improve your look and perception of you by others. Smiling is free and a must-have accessory to complete any outfit; so be generous with your smiles today. If you should see someone not wearing a smile, dig deeply, and give them one of yours to wear! Help us spread more smiles across the miles, America!"

~Cee Cee Sneed, Co-Author & NABE Pinnacle Book Achievement Award Recipient for Americans Saving Ourselves Together: How to Thrive in the 21st Century

The Inspiration for Our Music

Inspire means to breathe in. We have been breathing in the inspiration of Spirit, the Holy Spirit that is the Executive Will of God, since before we met. There are many ways to say this in this world, so please accept the essence of what we are saying. After we met, we developed together exponentially with the Inspiration of God and continue to grow to become One with All.

Our music and lyrics represent what many people are sensing and feeling but perhaps can't find the words or will to express. We see our music as inspirational, motivational, comforting and biographical at the same time. People have told us they feel like they are breathing in a breath of fresh air when they listen to us perform. It makes them smile, release some stress and become happier human beings.

A Healing Connection

    Just prior to when Daya met Chris, he was living at the Candee Hotel in Philadelphia at 21st and Chestnut. A flea bag hotel if there ever was one. It was full of interesting characters and among them was an old man who was constantly in pain.

    Being on a spiritual quest, Chris wondered why this man was suffering and asked the Creator why he couldn't be healed by Chris' laying his hands on him. He remembered a promise in the Bible that this could be done by those who believed. He got up the nerve to try and spent a quiet session with the man praying silently and placing his hands over the spots where there the pain was strongest.

Magical Encounter

Soon thereafter, he had a magical encounter with a musician who was playing music in the subway. As it was, Daya was a new member of the band that this musician was forming along with others. She embodied the healing power that Chris imagined when he tried to heal the old man. Chris and Daya connected with their music, their spirituality, their daily dreams and love of health and healing. They both shared an interest in Yoga. They began to write songs together which continues to this day, thirty-two years later.

Daya writes, "I used to offer distant healing to my Dad who was ill and he lived in Cincinnati, OH while I lived in Wilmington DE. I hadn't had any training for doing this type of healing; I just felt in my heart that I could. I'd draw a picture of my Dad and let that act as a surrogate for his physical and spiritual body. I would apply the energy that I felt through my hands and focus sending it through my mind to a cyst on right hemisphere of my Dad's head and to his heart.

It wasn't until ten years later that I would actually be attuned and certified to teach Usui Reiki and use this Universal light force energy to heal myself, family, friends and soon clients. I practiced spiritual healing and have been trained in Reiki, Matrix Energetics, BodyTalk, and Rebirthing along the way.

I had already been studying Hatha Yoga with my teachers, Professor Yogi Bharat Gajjar and Amrit Desai and meditating about 10 yrs before meeting Chris. I had started getting dreams that presented songs to me and the chords were shown to me in my dreams. One of my elementary teacher friends named Dan suggested I should put my lyrics on a lyric sheet. Eventually he suggested, 'why don't you learn to play guitar to accompany yourself?' I took a few lessons, but mostly taught myself. I met Chris while I was playing music with the Street Players on 16th and Chestnut Street in Philadelphia, PA.

Together Chris and I developed a musical style that emphasizes soaring harmonies, inspiring lyrics, and syncopated rhythms that has its roots in our street playing days in Philadelphia and surrounding boroughs.

More recently, we have performed with the SkyEarth Orchestra, a world influenced symphonic rock band that incorporates the original music of Steve Reel, Chris and myself. We performed with Cathie Reel on keyboards, percussion and Bodhran, Eddie Joiner on drums, percussion and mandolin and Cliff Shooker as bassist and saxophonist. We were joined by Larry 'Z.' on violin and James Thomas on didgeridoo.

New Opportunities

At one point in our musical journey, we were asked by a friend if we would like to perform at a community center in Maine for the locals. We accepted and drove up to Maine one weekend in the middle of winter and performed for a great crowd in a large auditorium. Afterwards, we were invited to stay as guests of our host in his farmhouse outside of town. I distinctly remember him showing us around as he went out to check on the sheep in the barn that night to be sure they were OK. The temperature was well below zero, so

Daya and I said goodnight and headed up to the bedroom, noticing the temperature drop as we moved further and further away from the wood stove in the kitchen. We crawled under the covers and strived to keep each other warm all night. The next morning our host had left for work, but he left this wonderful note. "You are both electric personalities and know the real secret of life- 'God will use you and continue to test you, as in the past' Psalms 118:24. I am so glad our stars touched." Daya kept these words in our scrapbook.

This in a nutshell may be what our musical journey has been about, just trying to let our light shine while facing obstacles along the way as well. Obstacles may not be the best word because we've come to understand that what might appear to be an impediment or obstacle is in actuality an opening to a new opportunity.

We were in a musical performance contest one time and based on our feeling and the audience reaction we knew we were going to do well. But due to politics we were completely overlooked. That seemed like a real issue, but as songwriters will do, we took this event and turned it into a song about overcoming adversity. The song begins, "Well we've got every reason in this whole wide world, to be down, but the Sun (Son) says keep moving on. We're like plants out of season, caught in a swirl, going round, but our hearts say we must be strong… Goodbye Heartaches…"

What Does Level Seven Mean?

We received the name **Level Seven** (changed to **aka Level Seven**) after sitting on the floor in the living room of our house on Phonetia Drive in Deltona, Florida meditating and listening when we knew a change was needed to the name of our duo. Not knowing it at the time, but soon after, an audience member at one of our shows gave us a card which explained the mystical meaning of the number seven. The basic idea is that it represents perfection in the earth dimension. You see it reflected in the seven days of the week, seven chakras in the etheric body and seven seals in the Bible. To reach the level seven, you are striving to manifest perfection on the earth plane in your daily living. Our name **aka Level Seven** incorporates that meaning, not only for ourselves but also for everyone. We all graduate from level one to level seven and then start again always learning more and more.

We are the offspring of musical parents. Chris' mom sang and his dad played the piano. My mom sang and my dad played the ukulele, guitar, piano and sang. My dad used to listen to records by Dave Brubeck, Frank Sinatra, Perry Como, Nat King Cole, Tony Bennett and other great artists of that time period.

Chris's Brief Musical Bio

As part of this *Smile America* project, I was asked to write a biography of my musical life. I got in touch with the brain cells that still retained such information and put together this brief recollection. I couldn't cover everything, but I did my best to help you get a picture; and decided to use the first names of those involved to protect the innocent. So here it goes......

Little did I know what a big event it was when I took my guitar out of retirement and headed down into the Philadelphia subway. It was February and the air was frigid, which made it hard for his fingers to move when playing the guitar, but there he was, a lone musician, sitting on a concrete bench in front of the tiled wall, wearing gloves with the tips of the fingers cut off so he could play the guitar. His case was open for the passers-by to throw in their spare change. I stepped outside my comfort zone and asked him if I could join in, since he was playing chords and singing songs that I recognized. This pattern repeated itself for the next few days and soon we played regularly together. As the spring approached, there were warm days to go upstairs and play on the streets, and cold days in the subway.

Self-Imposed Cocoon

This was big step for me. I had decided a year before that I was too "addicted" to music, so I put my guitar aside and had only played music briefly since then for inspired praise, singing to God in my room. At the time, I was on a spiritual quest, having been guided to leave everything behind and move to Philadelphia, where I ended up living in a downtown fleabag hotel after mooching off my brother's hospitality and living in his apartment for a period of time. I call the hotel "fleabag" because of such things such as open holes in the floorboards, bathroom doors off the hinges, bugs everywhere, and generally decrepit conditions. My days were spent studying holy books and unraveling the mysteries behind them, in libraries, coffee shops and fast food restaurants. My nights were spent mostly in my room (with an occasional walk around town), listening to the sounds emanating from the next room, heated arguments at times and heated lovemaking at others. I was not a busybody, but the paper thin walls made it impossible to avoid. Across the courtyard, if you could call it that because the ground was littered with debris, occasionally you could hear the sounds coming from that side of the building, a loud shouting match, a TV or music blaring, or the sound of an empty beer or wine bottle as it hit the cement below. Out of this self-imposed cocoon, I took small steps back into the world of music.

My interest in music started when I was young. I remember our family gatherings, my dad would play the piano, old songs from the 30's and 40's and before, such as "Lida Rose" and the "Birth of the Blues", or "We ain't got a barrel of money". My mother would stand next to him at the piano and sing harmony. Aunts and uncles and cousins would sing along as well with their parts. My parents signed me up for piano lessons with an elderly (to me) lady who forced me to read sheet music and tapped out the beat. Mistakes were frowned upon.

An Electric Guitar Pilfered

I endured through most of elementary school until one Christmas as a teenager when my brother Jim got an electric guitar. I became fascinated with that instrument and pretty much took it over from him and played it as often as I could. This was the time when Rock and Roll came into our house. We bought records and borrowed from our friends. Over the next few years, we heard the Beatles, Led Zeppelin, Cream, the Animals and I loved the sounds. Our neighbor brought a CSNY album and I spent hours listening and trying to play along. I learned some chords on the guitar and my brothers and I formed a "band" which played in the playroom. We also joined kids in the neighborhood to jam in a friend's basement.

During high school, I became friends with one of the free thinking nuns at my neighborhood Catholic Church who needed musicians for the folk mass and soon I was playing guitar with my friend Bob to lead the congregation in songs. We sat on chairs in the front left corner of the church, next to the confessional and in front of the altar. This was the basement church, more modern and contemporary than the traditional church on the floors above. The participants tended to be more open minded renegades. I learned sing-along songs with a folk, popular, contemporary beat.

My guitar went with me to Harvard College, and I spent many long hours listening to music and learning songs by Jimi Hendrix and The Allman Brothers, among others. I was on the crew team during my freshmen and sophomore years, but when I became a junior I decided that I needed to spend more time with music. I jammed regularly in another dorm (house) with a friend named Phil. I was becoming adept at learning how to play by hearing. I majored in English, but music was my passion.

After graduation, I decided that I would to take guitar lessons. I followed up on an ad and found Mike, a finger picking-slide guitar folk style player. He taught me a lot about using my right hand to pick. I shut myself in my parent's bathroom for hours to practice Traverse picking and listen to the sound bounce off the tiled walls. Mike and his wife moved to Arkansas. I rode buses there from Massachusetts to visit them and see the Ozark Mountains. While I was there, he invited me to perform a song on 12 string guitar at a community talent show. That was among the most nervous moments of my life, but I somehow made it through the song. My guitar lessons continued back in Massachusetts with a brief stint studying jazz and blues guitar. I began to perform songs, singing with my guitar for family, friends and anyone else that didn't walk away.

I got a job as a youth counselor at a neighborhood center in Dorchester, Mass. I spent most of my time leading athletic events, but also started a guitar group with some of the kids. Through this group I met an excellent flute player named Kathy who was a friend of the family of one of the guitar students. We formed a duo called Body and Soul. We got a job for the summer playing music in the lounge of a night club in Plymouth, Mass.

Gangsters and Gashes

An amazing event happened on the last weekend we were there that introduced me to a darker side of life and the music business. The older brother of one of the students in my guitar group was the lead guitarist in a rock and roll band that performed in the night club adjacent to the lounge where I was performing. We went over to see him perform after we finished our last gig. At the end of the night, a shouting match broke out between some of the inebriated guests. Things got out of control and one of the people broke his glass on the table and held it jagged edge out in a threatening position. My impression was that the man was unaware what he was doing, being drunk and hardly able to stand up, and relatively harmless, but one of the bouncers, who was also a regular in our lounge, ran up to the man and quickly in experienced fashion pulled out a switchblade and cut the man's face in an X pattern. Blood was everywhere.

The club cleared out fast and the crowd I knew headed over to a party at a local house. One other female guest and I were speaking out about what had just happened but everyone else was being silent. Pretty soon, the bouncer who had done the slashing arrived at the party and made his way over to me. With threatening words and attitude he told me to keep quiet about what I had just witnessed.

The next morning, I went to pick up my pay at the lounge (which also served brunch on Sunday mornings) and the owner was there, along with the crew and bouncer fellow. It hit me like a light between the eyes that these were gangsters running this whole complex and my bouncer acquaintance was a hit man. The vibes were intense, but I got my pay, got in my car and drove off, not looking back.

Click Fast Forward

Fast forward and there I was, standing on the streets of Philadelphia playing music with the Street Players, a collection of two male guitarists (me being one), an African percussionist, a flute player/singer and a beautiful guitarist/singer named Daya. I knew something very special was in the works. Daya and I would talk during breaks and we found that we shared a love of God, dreams and music. We fell in love and spent an eventful period until the cold weather came back, performing music on the streets during the day, sleeping in our apartment at night until our rent money was stolen by one of the band members. Then we slept under parked cars at night and eventually found an abandoned building where we could sleep.

The Street Players had other differences and went our separate ways, but Daya and I stayed together and soon we were married. We lived in Bucks County and had day jobs at a wood factory, making antique style phones. We would perform music as the duo, *Abraham's Seed*, wherever we could, on the streets, colleges, clubs or at festivals, sometimes taking the train to Philadelphia with our guitars and amps in tow.

One Chance to Be Chosen for Folk City

Though our home base was Philadelphia, we had heard about Folk City in New York and decided to go. We hitched a ride to New York City. We found the place but no one had told us the procedure for getting to perform there.

We met another musician who told us that we could put our name in a basket to be selected to perform by luck of the draw. We had to come back at a certain time and hope that our name was picked out of hundreds of names. We couldn't wait a week to be picked, so we only had one chance to be there by being chosen... and we were.

A friend of Daya's from Rider University, Monetta, lived in New York and was supportive and appreciative of what we'd accomplished to be there. She came to see us perform that night and took a photo of us. We still have it.

She invited us to stay with her that night, fed us and as we were on our way out the door the next morning, she bent down and slipped some money into Daya's sock. It was a twenty dollar bill. We had no money before that.

We reconnected with my family in the Boston area and decided to move there. They met Daya for the first time and opened up their hearts to receive us. We migrated through a series of living spaces in the Boston area, writing songs, performing, making a life and gaining friends and "fans".

We joined with like-minded musicians to form the musician's co-op, *Good Company Productions*, helping each other out with all aspects of performance and the business of music. Our first EP, *Sides of Love*, was produced with the help of our friend Jic, of Chicken Coop Productions, and distributed by *Good Company Productions*. We also joined with other songwriters as part of the *New England Songwriter's Association*, having some amazing all night music parties and putting on an annual concert at the Hatch Shell in Boston.

To supplement our musical income, Daya and I caught on with a country band. We named ourselves *Raindance* and performed throughout the area. We played everywhere with the band and as a duo, at colleges, universities and local clubs and we were radio guests as well. We became regulars on weekend nights at The Carriage House in Ipswich, MA and performed regularly at the Nameless Coffeehouse in Cambridge, MA.

We Can See Restored Prosperity

We bought our first home in Ayer, Mass. While doing laundry at a laundromat one day several years later, Daya noticed an ad on the bulletin board about a home for sale in Deltona, FL. We decided to visit it while on vacation in Orlando and through a series of serendipitous events ended up moving to Florida. With a new home came a new name, received in meditation, *Level Seven* (later changed to *aka Level Seven*).

I had started recording our music years before by playing directly into a 2-track recorder and later a 4-track cassette recorder. We also spent time in several studios and my interest was piqued in the recording process. Daya knew this, of course, and one year her birthday present was to help me sign up for recording school. I enrolled in the Audio Recording Technology Institute. This opened up a whole new world and over time I built up a fully equipped reel to reel home recording studio, which is now computer based. Our

CD *Level Seven* was recorded there. Most of the initial pre-production work on our songs is done in this home studio. I enjoy having the time to follow the process of trying things to see if they work, and putting the pieces of a song together to find how they blend together to make it whole.

Metaphysics and MIDI

While at ARTI, I took a class in MIDI. I resonated with the teacher's metaphysical, creative approach to sound and music. In one class, he talked at length about vibration, breaking down how everything is a wave form of vibration and how light is an octave waveform of sound waves. I had become interested in new thought and metaphysics years before, and I was astounded to hear this stuff in the context of MIDI and recording engineering.

After ARTI, I had basically been out of touch with the teacher, Steve Reel, when a few years later, I contacted him and found he was interested in putting a Celtic/world music/symphonic rock band together to perform the music from his CD *Celtic Knights*. He was looking for a keyboard player. Remember my piano lessons as a child? Although I consider guitar my primary instrument, I'm still a decent keyboard player, particularly in the context of rock and pop music. So I offered to join and soon Daya and I became part of what was to become the *SkyEarth Orchestra* with Steve and Cathie, eventually joined by our long time musical friend Eddie on drums and mandolin, Cliff who dedicated himself to mastering the intricate changing bass parts, Larry on violin, and occasionally James on digeridoo. We were also performing with Steve and Cathie as *Steve Reel and The Reels*, a rock/Celtic/variety cover band. Steve also helped me to master our first CD, *Level Seven*.

Daya and I continued to write songs and perform as *aka Level Seven*. We found that the relaxed, laid back island feel found in parts of Florida fits our music and life-style. Previously, Daya had developed an interest and also skills as a spiritual healer, and began writing children's and self-help metaphysical healing books. Her latest book, *Americans Saving Ourselves Together: How to Thrive in the 21st Century* was a collaboration of a group of female authors from around the country.

A Synchronistic Meeting

One of the ladies had wanted to meet Daya for years. They met at a book signing and we all became quick friends. Inez lived in the next town over from us. She heard our music and offered to introduce us to a friend of hers whom she thought might be able to help us with our music.

Daya went to the meeting along with Inez, since I was working. After answering a couple of questions, signs were good that things were going to go well and soon we were working with Maurice Starr, a Grammy award-winning Producer, on our new CD, *Smile America*. He is the impetus for this story of our musical life that you are now reading. One of the seven authors of *Americans Saving Ourselves Together: How to Thrive in the 21st Century*, Cee Cee Sneed, wrote a beautiful chapter with a section subtitled, *Smile America*. Daya was inspired to write a song based on that theme and I took up the challenge as well. So the songs *Smile America* and *America Smiling* were born. As I write the words of this brief bio, I'm listening on my iPod to the backing tracks of the *Smile America* CD that we're currently mastering. I'm enjoying this music as something of a culmination and also the latest stage of my musical journey. I hope you will enjoy it too.

Daya's Journey

As a child of separated parents, we were cared for by my mom. My dad made sure he always lived in nearby areas so we could go visit him on the weekends and longer during the summer months. He was wonderful. He was always fun to be with, loving, peaceful, happy and calm. He would play his ukele when we were visiting him, sing us songs he learned in the Navy and play his guitar while listening to his albums of soft music. My mom made sure we all had music lessons of our choice, which was a piano for my sister Dede and I and clarinet for my brother Lee. Through the power of manifestation, Mom attracted an upright piano for us to practice on and it was perfect for us. I loved being in the presence of the music my dad played on his record player. He was an artist so he'd be doing his oil colored painting sometimes while the music played for all of us to enjoy.

I stopped taking piano lessons by the time I got to middle school (junior high) at a certain point because it became too complicated for me (in my mind). I didn't get involved with music anymore until after my first son was born. I elected to resign my job at E. I. DuPont Nemours in

Wilmington, DE after taking a break for maternity leave. I started teaching in the Head Start Program and began "hearing" music and lyrics to write. I knew one of the teachers at the school who taught music at the elementary levels and shared my songs with him. I asked him if he would write the lyric sheets for me and the chords of the songs as I would sing into a tape recorder and he'd transcribe the chords over the notes. He said yes.

Why I Learned the Guitar

Eventually after somewhere around 10 sheets of music he got this great light bulb idea to share with me. He said, "Daya, why don't you learn how to play the guitar and then you could accompany yourself?" I thought it was a great idea. Who was going to teach me? I found a teacher and he happened to be a famous teacher who had written a well-known series of guitar books for students of various levels. My ex-husband was to come home early enough so I could leave my infant son with him, and I'd head of to be on time to class.

This arrangement didn't work out for me as he often didn't get home on time on purpose. My teacher told me he could not teach me if I didn't consider it important enough for me to be there on time for lessons. He didn't want to hear any excuses. I was late two times out of about 8 lessons and that was the end of my training. But, I had a desire so strong that I practiced everything he taught me every day for hours so that my fingers got calloused and painful. I taught myself new chords from the book I had purchased from him. I was helped by my music teacher friend to figure other things out if I got stuck and eventually I was able to sing my songs and accompany myself very well.

Soon I was being interviewed because of the concerts I started giving in the community. I found my photo was in all the county newspapers advertising my upcoming gigs on a regular basis. I found places everywhere that wanted to have me perform, i.e. during intermissions of plays, church functions in neighboring localities and malls where they had my name in large letters on the marquee. This all took place in the Wilmington, DE area and as far away Media, PA. Sometimes I'd play for dinner, sometimes for tips but mostly for a set fee that I negotiated with the managers.

"Pack Your Belongings and Leave Your Security Behind."

I divorced from my older son's dad and continued performing, writing and learning more and more chords. While my boy was a toddler, I had gone to post graduate school to get a degree in Early Childhood Education so that I could get an increase in pay and more responsibility. After he turned about eight years old, his dad got custody of him. I had heard in a vision one night to leave all my financial security behind me and go for making a living doing music. I woke up the next morning and wanted confirmation so I asked for another sign. I was led to a Bible verse which told me to pack up all my belongings and leave my financial security behind me. I don't know exactly what that verse is today but it was the sign I had asked for.

My full story is told in *The Only Way Out Is In: The Secrets of the 14 Realms to Love, Happiness and Success! http://www.padaran.com.* I went to England to perform at some restaurants that I had played at during a previous trip. I was not allowed into Heathrow Airport after I got off the plane. The security people told me that I had to have a letter stating I was the employee of these restaurants as an entertainer, otherwise I was being shipped back right away to the US. I never got pass the turnstiles. I was given fare back to US and started my career back in Philadelphia, PA, where I had been raised.

I stayed with my mom for about two months when I had to be evicted because she was living in a government subsidized apt rental due to her income level. She was not allowed to have anyone living with her or she'd lose her apartment.

I went to an audition in Philadelphia at one of the clubs and met two other musicians both applying. One was a flute player and the other a guitarist. They told me that they play in the subway when it's cold above ground and earn a living performing down there. They invited me to come join them anytime. Little did I know when I met them that I would need to refer to that invitation two weeks later after I had to leave my mother's place on Feb. 14, 1979. I had a feeling in my heart I should store that information away for later.

The Trek to Homelessness

I packed my things and was then homeless as I went to find them in the subway. They saw my sad face and asked me what was going on. I told them of my plight of being homeless. They told me right away that I could stay with them. They had a small room and I could sleep there after we finished playing for the day. They had a bed, a dresser, one chair and a closet when we got to their West Philly spot. One volunteered to sleep on the wooden chair; we took the mattress off the bed and put it crunched up between the apt door and foot of the wrought iron bed frame. I slept on the box spring with my clothes on. I had no fear because I knew God had provided this haven for me, however humble, and I would be watched over. They were very protective over me. I stayed there probably 3-4 days when their landlord thought I was a prostitute, the furthest thing from the truth, and told them I had to leave or they would be kicked out.

We had earned about $15 the next day among the three of us. They said they would share their money to give me $7 so I could stay at the YWCA. It was clean but about the size of a small prison cell like you might find on death row. There was a community bathroom. I felt claustrophobic and could not go back there. I draw a blank as to where I slept from there on until I met Chris later in February of that year. He allowed all of to crash in his downtrodden hotel room at the Candee Hotel, 21st and Chestnut St. It's been since torn down.

Our Romantic, Synergistic Meeting to Now!

Early in our life together as musicians, we played at a theatre in Camden NJ and didn't get paid for the gig. One of the workers at the theatre saw our predicament and offered to put us up for the night since we didn't have a place to stay. The next day he gave us a wonderful book about love as we were leaving. Two days later, when we needed some money for food and didn't have any, we opened the book and started to read it when we found a $5 bill as a book marker. Daya cried with a heart full of thanks.

Prior to this experience in Camden, NJ, we had hitched a ride to Atlantic City to talk to clubs about playing music there. We met a female casino worker who invited us to stay at her place for the night. When we arrived to her place, she had arranged for Chris to sleep with her in a pristine bed with a white canopy and Daya was to sleep in another room that was like a closet. She clearly had ulterior motives so we opted to leave and ended up sleeping under the boardwalk on the sand with our blanket and two guitars. The song *Under the Boardwalk* takes on a whole new meaning for us because of this remembrance.

In our travels, a humble man introduced himself to us as Frisco Bowman, an old-timer guitarist, at a Burger King Restaurant in Lower Manhattan. He saw our guitars and that was our introduction to this great man. He gave us some tips; one was to never let anybody touch our guitars. If someone asks your wife if they can play her guitar, she needs to tell them, "My husband will not allow me to have anyone else to touch it." That way the responsibility was on my husband and they could not argue with that. He told us many other things based on his experiences in the music business.

One time in Cambridge after one of our performances at the Nameless Coffeehouse, an audience member ran into me in the woman's restroom. She told me that upon hearing about our life together which seemed so fascinating, that we ought to consider writing a book about our lives. I never forgot that encounter and what I told her. I said, "I will and I think you are right." I did do that with my book, *The Only Way Out Is In: The Secrets of the 14 Realms to Love, Happiness and Success!* That is now an award-winning book that has reached a worldwide audience.

Essentially, we are both dedicated to reminding everyone how much fun it is to smile, to laugh, to giggle, hoot and holler and roll on our sides or backs laughing with glee and sharing our joy through our music. We want to see you smile, America!

You can see that the beginning of our distinctive musical journey together was synchronized by events that brought both of us to Philadelphia, PA. As our song, "Soulmates", describes it, *"She knew she would know him by the way he smiled; he knew she would be fun just like a little child..."*

In one of my interviews along the way, I share what I mentioned before, how I left my secure teaching job to follow my musical dream after being guided through a vision during the night. These were the words that I heard in my vision, "You must burn all the bridges behind you, pack your belongings and pursue music." I have continued to be guided by dreams, inspired to write songs through dreams, hearing and seeing songs being performed in the dreams, and being shown chords to play by the performers in my dreams. I, along with Chris, have been shown how to interpret our dreams through the messages received in them. We have used this information on a daily basis to help with our direction and decisions, also being shown to share this information in the dream workshops that we have taught.

Back in Philadelphia, I was performing music on the street with two other performers. Chris "wandered" by and began to come back on a regular basis. He soon became a member of the band and "The Street Players" was formed, performing day and night with our unique "acoustic funk" sound to crowds on South Street and Chestnut Street in Philadelphia to New Hope in Bucks County.

Where Do We Sleep Tonight?

The band eventually broke up, but our relationship continued. One of the band members took it upon himself to steal our rent money. He tried to make it look like we were robbed but we knew otherwise. We asked him about the money but he denied it. A period of homelessness ensued as the result of having no rent money, but we stuck together. We stayed in a condemned, abandoned building with no running water, no electricity, rotten floors and "critters". We slept in parks, on park benches, taking turns sleeping and keeping watch over our guitars. We slept under boardwalks as we mentioned earlier and under parked cars of apartment complexes. We'd ask to be awakened by Spirit before any car owners had to drive off for work. Our two guitars and our blankets were under the cars. We'd get freshened up as best we could at fast-food restaurants. We'd play for money donated by passers-by or for food donated by kind-hearted restaurant owners who allowed us to play for the patrons inside their restaurants. We always made sure that each of us saved ninety-nine cents for breakfast at a Greek diner the next day.

Hidden Resources

Somehow, money was provided out of "nowhere" when we needed it. Daya received $1600 from her teacher's retirement fund, which she wasn't expecting. This supported the band members for several months. When the weather started to cool, we moved to Doylestown and landed jobs working in a wood factory. This supported us during the winter. Chris later worked as a taxi driver. All the while we continued to play and perform music. We received a check from a settlement on the sale of her former house by Daya's ex-husband. When not working, since we now had an address, Daya was able to receive food stamps and welfare for a short time. We were learning that there were many avenues through which a person could be prospered.

During the previous summer in Philadelphia, we fell in love and soon were married. The story about that is told in detail in Daya's book, *The Only Way Out Is In: The Secrets of the 14 Realms to Love, Happiness and Success*! http://www.padaran.com

We visited Philadelphia several years after this eventful summer. We "coincidently" ran into the former band member who had stolen our rent money, while walking down Chestnut Street where we used to perform. He held his head down in shame, but we spoke to him anyway. He told us how his luck had gone sour ever since that day and he asked us to forgive him. We told him we had forgiven him years ago and that brightened and lightened his face and heart.

Migrating to the Boston area, we joined with the songwriter co-op, New England Songwriter's Association, and with Good Company Productions. Good Company distributed our first EP, *Sides of Love*, as Chris mentioned before. We were nominated for awards in songwriting and vocal harmony by the Massachusetts Country Music Awards Association (MCMAA) and we performed guitar and vocals with the country band *Raindance*. Our music continued to evolve and we were led to head south to find a home in Central Florida.

The Genesis of Smile America

We fell in love with the warm sub tropical breezes in our Florida home. This drew us to a style of music that incorporated our country folk-rock and Philadelphia street music sound and added a relaxed island feel. Out of this was born our first CD, *Level Seven*. We performed throughout Florida as a duo and also with Steve Reel and the Reels and the SkyEarth Orchestra, as keyboardist and guitarists while offering background vocal harmonies. The former performed cover and Celtic rock and the latter had a unique symphonic rock and world music sound.

After a series of events related to an economic depression in the country, Daya received an idea that was the answer to a prayer she had asked Spirit. She wanted to know what part she could play in helping her fellow Americans to thrive during the current economic woes instead of just barely surviving to stay above water. She was led to gather six authors who happened to live coast to coast to co-author a spectacular, transformative book entitled *Americans Saving Ourselves Together: How to Thrive in the 21st Century*.

One of the chapters in the book has a subtitle, *Smile America,* and wonderfully deals with being happy, positive and carrying a smile in daily living as a way to thrive and be successful in all areas of life. This was contributed by one of the seven authors, Cee Cee Sneed. Daya was particularly impressed with this chapter, and she felt that "Smile America" would make a good title for a song. She began working on her idea and eventually with some help from Chris, the song *Smile America* came together. Chris and Daya performed this song at the book-signing for *Americans Saving Ourselves Together*, which is where Inez and our friends Drs. Nalani and her husband Dr. Phil Valentine, "Sunnu" also heard it. They were all impressed with the song and thought it was a hit. It stayed in Inez' mind, which inspired her to put us in contact with Maurice Starr,

Working with Maurice has brought us to a new level in terms of production, arrangement, quality and we feel it is reflected in our CD, *Smile America.* He has been a master in subtly bringing out the best in us. When Chris was listening to the early drafts of Daya's song, he gave himself a personal challenge to write a song around the same theme. This became the song, *America Smiling*, on our current CD.

The apparent irony in all of this is that while the authors of the book were spread from coast to coast across our country, the principles that came together to make our new CD, that being Inez, Maurice, Daya and I were all in local adjacent towns in Central Florida. I think there is a message here that the larger change we all are looking for will start close to home, one by one, little by little.

Tour Map of Our Musical Journey
Life Events

1979 Met on Chestnut Street, Philadelphia, PA. Performed music on streets winter to autumn.

1979 Moved to Doylestown PA in November.

1980 Moved to Boston MA area. Moved 9+ times in the span of 5 years and had at least as many cars.

1983 Heard about Farmer's Home Mortgage Administration while buying our VW Bus. Bought our first home in Ayer, MA with no money.

1986 Moved to Central Florida after seeing the Deltona house during our vacation.

1994 In the same week of December, we bought our historic home Enterprise, FL., Chris lost his day job, and our baby son, Joseph came into our lives.

2001 Daya's book, **Super Vita-Minds, How to Stop Saying I Hate You to…Yourself**, is published.

2003 Bought our current home in Deltona, FL which borders a nature sanctuary, home to Gopher Tortoises, a few Rattlesnakes, Raccoons, Coyotes and endangered Florida Scrub Jays.

2004 Celebrated 25 years being married having a memorable formal re-dedication ceremony attended by family and friends.

2008 Daya's book, **The Only Way Out Is In, the Secrets of the 14 Realms to Love, Happiness and Success!** is published.

2009 Daya co-edits award-winning book **Americans Saving Ourselves Together, How to Thrive in the 21st Century**, in collaboration with authors from across the country.

Music Events

1979 Performed on South Street and also Chestnut Street with the "Street Players" in Philadelphia.

1979 Hitched to New York to perform at Folk City. Proved that a way can be made if you act on faith.

1981-1985 Joined Good Company Productions, New England Songwriters Association and Massachusetts Country Music Awards Association. Honored for songwriting and vocal harmony.

1981 Awarded for songwriting and vocal harmony at Boston's 2nd Annual Celebrity Awards Show, John Hancock Building. Also performed throughout the area: Hatch Shell, Boston/Cambridge area popular night spots, clubs, radio, festivals, weddings and colleges.

1984 Our first ever EP **"Sides of Love"** is released.

1986-Present **"aka Level Seven"** duo performs throughout Florida at festivals, clubs, coffeehouses, concerts and private events and inspires millions (seen and unseen).

1989 **"You Are The Light"** video produced in Orlando in conjunction with *Full Sail Recording Studios*.

1992 Macy Chronicles is presented to the governor of the State of Florida, featuring **Forgotten Song** soundtrack by The Doolins.

1994-2005-Live performances by Chris and Daya at the Florida Folk Festival.

2001 Chris studies recording engineering and MIDI at ARTI in Orlando.

2004 Chris and Daya joined **Steve Reel and the Reels,** performing sweet Celtic rock and variety music extensively at festivals and venues.

2005 Members of the **Reels** join others to form **SkyEarth Orchestra**, developing an expansive symphonic world rock sound.

2005 CD **"Level Seven"** is released for worldwide distribution by **aka Level Seven**.

2009 We join Grammy Award- Winning Producer Maurice Starr to work on the **"Smile America"** project.

Humorous (in retrospect) Happenings

1979 Spring/Summer/Fall-competing with buses, commuters and sounds of the city to be heard as street players with acoustic instruments; someone always on guard to protect the money in the guitar cases.

1979 Autumn- Ride the train with Philadelphia commuters to perform at gigs with guitars and amps in tow. Back to the train by 12 midnight or we were on the streets for the night.

1983-1985 One of many temporary or part-time jobs that Chris had, to supplement musical income, was working as a car salesman at a small lot. The owner had no real interest in selling cars but just needed someone there so he could keep his used car license and tax write-off. When no customers were present, it was an excellent place to write songs and practice guitar while being paid.

1983 Depending on money from a scheduled gig to help with living expenses. Showed up at the club and the building was closed due to flooding. No-one had notified us.

1984 Driving uphill to a gig during the winter, heard a loud "pop". Chris went to the back to check. The spark plug had blown out of our VW bus engine. He found it on the street, screwed it back in by hand and we drove off as if nothing had happened. While driving to/from the Carriage House gigs during winter, we wrapped ourselves in blankets, not being able to use the hot air heat in our other VW hatchback because an exhaust leak would have asphyxiated us.

1986 Our van had broken down on a previous trip, so Chris parlayed his job at the used car dealer into a $300 dollar car that drove us to Florida. Like something out of the Beverly Hillbillies, we had the car packed to the gills and items strapped to the roof as we drove I-95 in tandem with our U-Haul truck from Boston to Deltona, Florida.

2006 Performing at an outdoor festival in Mt. Dora, FL., a sudden windstorm blows up and sends chairs flying, knocks over vendor tents, and blows over the tent that is protecting us onstage from the sun's heat. Vendors scramble to save their equipment and merchandise and we scramble to avoid getting knocked on the head by the poles from the tent. Since no-one was seriously hurt to our knowledge, we can look back and laugh, because it was a bizarre scene with things flying everywhere.

Reviews about our music:

"...They, Level Seven, possess captivating harmonies. A kind of blissful gentleness permeates their material, yet is never cloying". Steve Morse – Boston Globe, MA

"...Theirs is a winning performance. Her voice is a warm gravely alto, his a soft tenor." Thom Duffy, Orlando Sentinel, FL

"...An enchanting duo. Their vocal harmony is incredible!! Soft, searching and intense!" M.C.M.A.A., MA

"They are the best I've heard. I follow them whenever they're playing...can't wait for their CD." G. F.

"The music, voice and harmony are just beautiful!" C.J. FL

Some Awards & Nominations:

- Nominated Best Duo, *Massachusetts Country Music Awards Association*, Boston, MA Seven consecutive years
- Nominated Best Vocal Harmonies, MCMAA for seven consecutive years

- *Nominated Best EP "Sides of Love",* MCMAA
- Voted Best Original Song-2nd Annual Celebrity Awards Show
- Publishing Contract with :Jaclyn Publishing Co. Nashville, TN contract for *"Everybody Knows"*
- Video: - "You Are The Light" (1989)
- Abraham's Seed   EP "Sides of Love"-1982
- Level Seven CD – 2006
- **Musical score for "Macy Chronicles" -1995**
- **Smile America CD and book -2010**

Our Philosophy: Persistence, Patience, Passion, Faith and aligning with our Divine Presence is the key.

Move into your SMILING phase America

In this book, we've written down many things that we have done and have had a reason to SMILE about. These include things we have received that we are grateful for. Now we'd like to invite YOU to move into your SMILING phase and do your part to acknowledge that you have a lot to smile about. We want to share these exercises that follow for you to get busy with your part. And if everyone in America decides to do this, we'll see a happier America, ready to reconnect with the true essence of living, which is joy.

Exercise #1

- Draw a picture of a conference table first on letter size paper.
- Draw a large empty platter for food.
- Draw about 50 plates on this platter.
- On the plates write down quickly what gifts you have received from the Universe, God, and friends or given to yourself (like self-confidence, self-esteem, a friend, wonderful parents, someone who loves you for yourself, a new book, a fulfilling day at work, etc.).

On another piece of letter size paper

- Draw another conference table with plates
- Write down on the empty plates all the negative habits or situations you would like to release (like fear of whatever, jealousy, unhealthy traits, illness, unworthiness, resentments, difficult people, debts; in other words, whatever you desire to be free of and have it replaced with joy, happiness, success, and freedom).

Take the second paper and burn it, bury it, freeze it or toss it away into a trashcan to be released from your life. Dispose of it in a way that has the most meaning for you. Take the other paper, which contains your aspirations for joy, and put it in a place of power or special significance for you, such as a treasure box, altar, under a religious statue or in a natural setting by your favorite tree. Let this remain there until you have begun to allow yourself to enjoy who you were meant to be, innocent, powerful, creative, loving and giving.

Exercise #2

This is based on our experience while driving to Daya's mother's funeral and back home from the funeral, which could have been an extremely somber time, but spontaneously, became a way for us to release those feelings of sadness by writing about what we were seeing and feeling during the trip.

- Look at the things around you... be very observant. Start to write down a description and let your imagination take over.
- Use silly words, silly rhymes, words that you make up, and silly patterns within the sentences. Think like a child or Dr. Seuss.
- Examples of how we did this are found in Returning to The Source section.
- Do not censor yourself but let the words flow without questioning what you are writing. Allow yourself to have a belly laugh and extreme fun while you doing this.
- Be silly, immature, improper, uninhibited, spontaneous, in the moment and there are no rules to hold you back.

Allow your passions to come forth like playing your guitar, or learn to play one. Learn how to be the best you can be with practice, determination, patience and persistence. All the reasons to be smiling will be revealed to every American very shortly.

When you see us at a concert, give us your SMILE AMERICA, be happy, and be delighted that our hearts have touched for an *instant*.

Spiritual Guidance

We have listened to our spiritual guidance all our lives and have always been blessed by Spirit to lead us to a happy and fulfilled life together and with our children.

We hope this book inspires you to live your passion, to be an inspiration to others, help others to learn how to smile and be grateful for everything no matter if you are driving a truck, cleaning toilets for a living, picking up trash for the community, selling coffee at a Seven –Eleven or teaching, etc.

Try to do everything as if it matters because it does. If you are living your passion, you are following your dreams, being your dreams and sharing that love with others, lifting them up in spirit. Your smile will help America to Smile, again. It will turn someone's life around for the better. It will bring joy and laughter to them again just seeing you happy and smiling.

We know our passion, our music will make you smile because that is what we see happening when we perform our songs for and with others. Our music makes Us SMILE!

Message From Source

On 9/12/10, I was on way to Sanford, FL to pick up Joseph and Chris from their Sunday bike ride together. What I heard from Spirit while driving brought tears to my heart – a kind of proclamation to our book after the lyrics portion page of **Smile America**.

"In the beginning was 'Abraham's Seed' (our former Duo name), you, Chris, your marriage and your music. Your music and marriage was the seed and it was rooted in Heaven (your minds) and earth (your deeds, actions and faith on earth). Like your Amaryllis plant, is how your music is, sturdy, strong and beautiful. Your flower took two years to blossom for you – two years Is nothing in the whole scheme of things – there is no time – but your faith never would allow you to believe it would not blossom somehow. You did not discard it and say it will never blossom, what's the use in trying to keep hope.

Your music is the Amaryllis plant now that was the Abraham's Seed planted in fertile ground of your hearts. Your music is the flower of the Amaryllis plant that you have seen pop open. It is beautiful and like your plant, your music will be found everlasting, beautiful and awesome by millions of listeners as was planned from the beginning.

You are faithful children and you have already been rewarded by your faith. It is established and has been from the beginning of your accepting the truth within each other and recognizing each other as planned in your song "Soul Mates". Your son Joseph will be performing with you and he is to put his own take, rhythm, heart and soul into his part without you controlling what you think needs to take place. Your music has its own direction and Divine force within it and beyond what you think you see.

It is established in MY MIND and So It Is!"

Lyrics to Our Smile America CD
Copyrighted © 2010

Chris and Daya Devi-Doolin

America Smiling
Chris Doolin and Daya Devi-Doolin

*Born out of **Americans Saving Ourselves Together: How to Thrive in the 21st Century**, known as the ASOT Project, a collaborative book that Daya was involved with, this song was started by Chris, who saw the story of 2 people coming together as representing how we all rise up with help from each other in the land of opportunity.*

Chorus:
I can see America smiling,
Left behind is that fearful frown.
I can feel a new day dawning,
Gone are the days of looking down.

The only chance she saw to make a life was in L.A.
Folding towels, cleaning rooms she worked hard day by day,
Then gave in to fear and doubt.
She was down, on the street, looked about everywhere,
To feed her kids, find a place to stay.
Met a friend, she caught a break, found a job she liked.
She works downtown near where she stays.

Chorus:
I can see America smiling,
Left behind is that fearful frown.
I can feel a new day dawning,
Gone are the days of looking down.

He left the gang, made a friend,
She was not from his world.
He knew this change was just what he needs.
They fell in love, head over heels, looking back no more,
Free and clear from past mis-deeds.

Chorus:
I can see America smiling,
Left behind is that fearful frown.
I can feel a new day dawning,
Gone are the days of looking down.
Smiling, smiling, smiling, smiling
                Smiling, smiling, smiling, smiling

I Know The Secrets
Daya Devi-Doolin
Chris Doolin

This song was written after Daya was watching a documentary about Native Americans and their cultural beliefs.

I know the secrets of the mountains
Of the desert and the stars
I know the message of the valleys
And the fire that is ours, with you… with you.
I know the rhythm of the ocean
And the laughter that it brings,
The wind is dancing devotion
As across the world it sings, to you… to you.

You encircle the four corners
Of the universe
Swirling clouds across the open skies
Sending moonbeams with your soft hands
Chasing shadows that fly by.

I crossed the border and surpassed time
Stirred love loose for you and me
We'll move together now in rainbow rhyme
As we sail the endless sea, to you…to you.

Instrumental then repeat chorus and verse

I Will Never Walk Alone
Daya Devi-Doolin and Chris Doolin

At a time when Daya wasn't feeling too strong emotionally, she was presented these words to inspire herself and lift herself up.

I will never walk alone, 'cause I have finally found my home
Ahhhh, what peace and joy I've found
And I will always be around you.

My Father's house is where I live
That's where I find the love to give
Ahhhh, what happiness I've found
And I will always be around you.

Though I travel far and wide through distant lands
You always take me by the hand
Sometimes the clouds may try to hide my way
But through your eyes, I see the Light of day

I will never be afraid, 'cause I am in His heart to stay
Ahhhh what peace and joy I've found
I will always be around you.

Never walk alone
Peace and joy I've found
In your heart to stay
Always be around

Make Up Your Mind
Daya Devi-Doolin and Chris Doolin

Daya used to work for a major electrical engineering company as a temporary office worker. She found many people were unhappy with their decision to be there so she wrote the basic words to this song as a way to inspire them to follow their dreams. This was done while on break or during downtime. Chris helped her with finishing the words and music.

Chorus:
Make up your mind, make up your mind, do what you want to.
Do what you want, do what you want, do what you want to.

Your dream is calling to you to catch it if you can.
I've seen it waiting for you exactly where you stand
Some will have advice to give you of what is best for you
Just listen to what you hear then you'll know what's true.
Chorus
Make up your mind, make up your mind, do what you want to
Do what you want to, do what you want, do what you want to.
Bridge:
Watch the man who's giving all his love away,
He takes time for living, giving love each day.
See the children playing, Laughter fills the air
Look at how they love life, living without care –
Without care
Chorus
Ending

Not My Job
Daya Devi-Doolin
Chris Doolin

Based on a relationship where you try to help someone but they continue to self-destruct. You conclude, It's Not My Job to pick up the pieces of your life any more.

Everybody knows that you're insane, it's true
Everybody knows you're not to blame, are you?
Everybody knows that no one's there for you
Everybody knows that no one cares for you, but me.

I see your heart is heading for the fan.
And all the pieces they fall down.
And even though it's set for free.
I am not about to stand around and
Chorus: It's not my job. It's not my job to watch you
        It's not my job to watch you falling
        It's not my job. It's not my job to watch you
        It's not my job, to watch you crawling

I don't want the pay. I don't like the pay.
And I don't want the pay today!
Chorus
Instrumental
Back into chorus

Let Me Explain (Not Too Late)
Daya Devi-Doolin
Chris Doolin

Two years ago, Daya watched Oprah interview Meg Ryan. Meg had taken a break from doing movies for a while because she had to find her place, her true self before she could continue onto anything else. What she learned about herself is explained in this song. Chris and I also incorporated what our parents taught us about being true to one's self. Daya was very happy and inspired to hear how Meg had allowed herself to come forth and be the person she truly is. Daya wrote this song that day. She kept the melody and tune in her head for two years until Chris was able to work on it with her after he heard Daya play the basic song. Meg said in the interview with Oprah (paraphrasing), "I don't have to be who you think I am, I don't have to be a star, I don't have to be who you want me to be, I just have to be who I am."

Let me see, if I can explain some things to you
They're hard to come by, but only life can bring them to you.
You don't have to be who they think you are
You don't have to be a star.
You don't have to be who they want you to be
You just have to be who you are.
Chorus:

It's not too late: let me see if I can explain
It's not too late: let me see if I can explain
It's not too late, not too late

When I was young, my mother she showed me what to do
I'm passing it on, the ageless baton, my love for you.
To listen and be wise
She opened up my eyes.
She taught me what to do
An now I'm showing you

Chorus:

Bridge:
Things I did not have the heart to share
No one cared, they were blind
Now the time has come to open up and pass the gift to you.

You are young. The whole world is there for you.
So much fun, people are there to care for you.
Find a place to start
Just open up your heart
Don't be afraid to share
And find someone who cares.

Chorus and end

Smile America
Daya Devi-Doolin   Chris Doolin

One of the co-authors of Daya's latest award winning book, **Americans Saving Ourselves Together: How to Thrive in the 21st Century***, Cee Cee Sneed wrote a chapter on being happy. One subtitle was Smile America and it was superb. It really stood out. One day, Daya was guided to write a song for Americans, humanity to be exact that exhorted to pick ourselves up together by being happy. We know that by being happy, you can create the impossible out of the unknown.*

If we don't try to help each other solve this mystery
We won't find out how very strong we are
The challenges well, they're all great, we know we can't be weak
Just put your helping hand in mind, we'll see.

Chorus:
It's time to Smile, Smile, Smile America
Holding onto what is dear and true.
And we will Smile, Smile, Smile America
For God has not forsaken me and you.

Bridge: Let all our tears and fears and sorrow just slip away
Don't watch the ground; just hold your head up high.
Let's do the very best we can and soon, we all will Know.
Nothing can defeat our hearts
Because our faith is strong! 2X

If we don't get this thing together, one by one we'll see
You and I need each other to be strong.
Traveling this road together, from sea to shining sea

Open up to what we all can be

Chorus
It's time to Smile, Smile, Smile America
Holding onto what is dear and true
And we will Smile, Smile, Smile America
For God has not forsaken me and you.

Chorus:
And we will Smile, Smile, Smile our whole way through
Holding onto what is dear and true
And we shall Stand Tall, Tall America
For God has not forsaken me and you.
For God has not forsaken me and you.
For God has not forsaken me and you.

Surrender
Daya Devi-Doolin
Chris Doolin

*Sondra Ray, an international best-selling author and Rebirther was Daya's inspiration here. She wrote a chapter in one of her books called Surrender. At a seminar that Sondra was giving, Daya and Sondra experienced a Holy Instant together for a brief moment and Daya could see the Universe through her eyes. Immediately upon leaving the seminar, Daya wrote the lyrics and music in her head. Daya and I worked out the arrangement of the music for our CD. The experience was in line with the teachings of **A Course in Miracles**. We dedicate this song to her. We found that when we surrender anxieties, fears and worries these will be replaced with joy, bliss and happiness. You will have made the right choice by surrendering.*

Verse
You don't have to feel alone, to run away and hide.
You may not see me always with you,
But I'll be there at your side.
You gain nothing keeping separate staying to yourself
Love is lost until you find it to share with someone else.

Chorus:
Surrender   (All your tears will fade away)
Together (Love is here for us to stay)
Surrender   (I am yours and you are mine)
Forever   (We are one in love's design)
Surrender (That's when we'll know love is true)

Together (You in me and me in you)
Forever   (We'll find love)

Peace comes easy when we forfeit
Forcing what seems right.
Giving up what doesn't count is a blessing in disguise.
You gain nothing keeping separate staying to yourself.
Love seems lost until you find it to share with someone else.

The Forgotten Song
Chris Doolin and Daya Devi-Doolin

Instrumental

*Inspired by a section in **A Course in Miracles** called The Forgotten Song (Chapter 21, page 415)*

"Beyond the body, beyond the sun and stars, past everything you see and yet somehow familiar, is an arc of golden light that stretches as you look into a great and shining circle. And all the circle fills with light before your eyes. The edges of the circle disappear, and what is in it is no longer contained at all. The light expands and covers everything, extending to infinity forever shining and with no break or limit anywhere. This is the vision of the Son of God, whom you know well. Here is the memory of what you are, a part of this, with all of it within, and joined to all as surely as all is joined in you. You know the ancient song, and know it well. Nothing will ever be as dear to you as is this ancient hymn the Son of God sings to his Father still."

The Phoenix
Chris and Daya Devi-Doolin

The myth of the Phoenix, a bird who rises from his own ashes to live again, can be applied to the world where people war within and without, yet hope holds on to belief that peace will prevail.

There are those in the world who hold to a view
That life is for love and living peace too.
But some of us don't know the purpose we are here
So we fight and we war to hold onto our fear.

Chorus:
But the Phoenix will rise from its ashes and hope will spring from despair.
The love will rise to the surface and peace will rein everywhere....Ooooo oooooo

The signs all around say the time it is near,
For men to put aside their hate.
We can change, change our lives, and put aside fear
For love it is never, never too late
Chorus
Ooooo oooo
    We hold these truths to be self-evident...That all men and women are created equal.

Tomorrow Is Now
Chris and Daya Devi-Doolin

We had a friend in our songwriter's group who fell in love with a guy who was younger than she was. She was afraid of being hurt and embarrassed about falling for him. She had a feeling it was too good to be true and it came to pass that they would part. She was devastated at the breakup and became sort of a recluse. It took a long time before she stopped being closed up in her bedroom but she did find her way out of it eventually with the support of her family and friends.

Every day, she'd sit all alone in her room
With just the sound of her ticking clock.
She was afraid of her life and afraid of dying
She was afraid of her fears and afraid trying.
She was afraid to taste the sun and afraid of crying
And she never saw the sunrise at sunset.

Chorus:
But tomorrow is now and here is the day
When she wore her tears like a dress
Tomorrow is now and gone is the day
When she knows there are no regrets.

There's no turning back, she's letting it go,
It's time to be free and she's letting it show
There's no turning back and there's nowhere to hide
She's starting it over, she's ready to fly.
Every day, she'd sit all alone in her gloom
Listening to the cold winter's rain.
She was afraid to try again and afraid of losing
She was afraid to risk again and afraid of moving
She was afraid to act on faith and afraid of choosing

And she never saw the sunrise at sunset.

Chorus:
But tomorrow is now and here is the day
When she wore her tears like a dress
Tomorrow is now and gone is the day
When she knows there are no regrets.

There's no turning back, she's letting it go,
It's time to be free and she's letting it show.
There's no turning back and there's nowhere to hide
She's starting it over, she's ready to fly.
She's starting it over,
She's starting it over,
She's starting it over, she's ready to fly, fly fly.

Springtime
Chris and Daya Devi-Doolin
Instrumental

Chris received the music for this song while vacationing with Daya in a cabin on the side of a mountain lake. Just imagine a stream flowing down from the heights.

Poetry by

*Chris Doolin, Daya Devi-Doolin,
Joseph Doolin and
Tyler R. Mitchell
Excerpts from:
Returning to the Source
&
Super Vita-Minds: How to Stop Saying I Hate
You...To Yourself*

Returning to The Source

Some of the poems in this section were co-written with my husband and partner Chris, my Kindergarten-aged son Joseph Doolin and oldest son Tyler Mitchell.

This entire section of poems is about Returning to the Source, the Source of our Innocence, the Source of our Spiritual nature and the Source of Transitioning.

My mother, Sallie T. Brown returned to the Source on June 22, 2000. As my family and I were driving to and from Philadelphia to lay her to rest, we started composing some of these dear poems. They made us laugh, and laugh and laugh some more. We were doing bellyache laughing. Tears were streaming down our faces. There were also some serious moments when I wrote my thoughts down.

This was very therapeutic for all of us to say the least. On the way home from Philadelphia as we were driving, my mother in Spirit asked to speak with me. As she did, I wrote her words down. They were included in my book, Super Vita-Minds: How to Stop Saying I Hate You…To Yourself. We dedicate this section in her memory.

Returning To The Source – Poems

Lines Seem Solid Here
Nothing to Do
What it was, I Forgot
Laughter in the Wind
Gift of the Spirit
Savor the Splendor
Sweet Nectar
A Trip to The Store
Fun in the Sun
Butterflies in the Attic
Wisdom Obeys Not the Fool
I Call You to The Door Of My Heart
Ringlets of Laughter
Shooting Stars
Pass me a Cup
Living the Life
We'll See about That
Free Breakfast Bar
Taxi Anyone?
Cheek and Beak
Back Seat Passengers
Puppet Master

Lines Seem Solid Here

The things that the world thinks it sees
Holds dear the images that seem.
Through darkened glass
To grab on tight
With gripping nails
And dripping fright.

Fear of death and
Fear of loss and
Fear of fear itself.
Fear of love and fear of hate
And fear of what has past.

The things the world thinks that it sees,
Make lines seem solid here.
But the darkened glass
When once removed,
Will reveal the Love of Him.
And the Light obscured but for a time
Will take the place of
Fear.

Nothing to Do

Have you ever gone to the zoo
And run into
A blue Emu
Who knew what to do
And said to you
Do you have a boo-boo?

Meanwhile the Gnu
Flew over to you
And said a-choo
Would you do a favor for Lou
The Kangaroo?
He doesn't have a clue
About what to do.

His cage is like a giant shoe
And he always cries boo-hoo
Being stuck in a shoe
With nothing to do,
Wouldn't you?

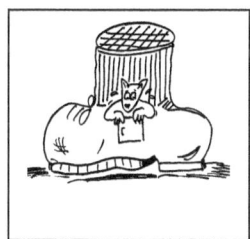

What It Was, I Forgot

I woke up this morning.
The sun was sure hot.
I went to buy a newspaper
And walk my dog Spot.

The circus was in town
 In a nearby plot.
We saw a giant cannon in the parking lot.
Spot broke free
And ran over in a trot,
Hopped inside the cannon
It went off with a shot.

He went sailing in the air like an Astronaut
And disappeared in the sky into a small black dot.
I went to go chase him, but my foot got caught
By the ankle of a contortionist tied up in a knot.

I tripped and fell, my nose landed on an apricot
Which smelled awful since it had started to rot.
I was hoping my efforts weren't for naught

lying face down on a smelly apricot.
Meanwhile, Spot had passed over a school where I had taught and spun wildly toward the ground in the town of Camelot.
He ricocheted through a window and landed in a pot
In the elegant café at the local Marriott.
The chef was making dinner, His brow was fraught.
His wife had thrown him out. He was sleeping on a cot.
When he opened up the pot, out jumped Spot.

He ran out the back door,
Past a car the chef had bought
And jumped into the stroller of a passing tiny tot.
It just so happened my sister, the one who owns the yacht
Was the owner of the stroller that housed the dog I sought.
She called me on her cell phone and said what she had got.

I hopped into a taxi and headed toward the spot.
Here we had our reunion, to hold back tears I fought.
As we walked home together,
I tried to remember what it was
That I Forgot?

Laughter in the Wind

I hear laughter in the wind.
Children's voices clamoring with Glee
Like sea gulls over a feast of oysters, Clams or bread.

The essence of their joy
Wraps around my heart
Like an umbilical cord connects a baby to life.
Now you can see me laughing as my laughter is carried
By the wind.

Gift of the Spirit

Joy is the gift of Spirit
To imprint its ecstasy upon the soul.
Joy is mystical love wandering
From cell to cell of the universe.

So, lift up the skirts of your heart.
Allow it to rush in
And take control over you, with laughter.

Savor the Splendor

Dust every piece of sadness from your heart.
Invite the Angel of Joy to carry you
To a place you've been to before
But forgotten.
Savor the splendor of the scent of laughter
For it will have transported you a far distance
By the time you will have returned.

Sweet Nectar

Imbibe with me
The sweet nectar
Of my natural Self.
Let it enfold you with its softness.
Let it make the cells of your heart Beg for more.

There is nothing like it you know.
Don't run away and try to hide.
It wants to make you drunk with Peace.
Come taste the elixir of happiness.
It's free.

A Trip to the Store

Sometimes it's a real chore
When you have to go to the store
And buy some more
Of what you are looking for
And listen to that talkative bore
In aisle four
While the clerk sweeps the floor
And the manager gives a tour
To Mister and Mrs. Apple Core
Who are chief investors
Not being poor
Making their money from iron ore in
Labrador.
And after you find what you're looking for
You pay for it
And walk out the door.

Fun in the Sun

Having fun lying in the sun
With a hot dog and a bun.

Suddenly, a gangster
On the run
Firing his gun
At no one
Chased by a ton
Of policemen,
Tripped over a geranium
While back-peddling
Through a palladium.
My son yells
There's a giant chicken
On the water tower.
And everyone even the Nun
Laughed and started having fun
Lying in the sun by the
Statue of Napoleon.

Butterflies in the Attic

Caught there by a draft in the wind.
Or did they arrive on purpose because
They sensed the memories of
Joy and Laughter who reside there?

Wisdom Obeys Not the Fool

Wisdom stands tall, centered and balanced,
Not wavering at the slightest bit of
Scurrying of anxious thoughts or fears.
Wisdom is comfortable in the clothes that it wears,
For It knows who It is.
The fool says to Wisdom; let's play, for we are the same.
Wisdom says fine,
I'll choose the rules and pick the games.

I Call You to the Door of My Heart

I look at and call to you day by day
To Come and bathe in the creeks of my Beingness.
Enjoy the splendor of my cradling arms that are soft,
energizing and Serene.

But I AM simply a faint memory as you walk the cement jungles you have created
In my stead;
Believing it will bring you peace.

Come be renewed in my rivers, my Mountains and my forests.
Come dance with me once more.
I call you to the Door of my heart
For Our love is waiting to be exchanged not ignored.

Ringlets of Laughter

Come press your heart to my heart.
Feel the molecules of our joy
Pass across our invisible bond of light,
Gathering moonbeams, ringlets of laughter and cosmic rays
as they Explode.

Listen to the fairies dipping their feet in the sprinkling stardust that
Fills the bowls of our hearts.

Shooting Stars

Shooting stars.
What are they shooting?
Rays of laughter, rays of hope, rays of wonderment,
Expectancy,
Childhood innocence.
Shooting stars.
What are they shooting?
AWWWWWE mixed with Joy!

Pass Me a Cup

Pass me the bowl of effervescence.
Pass me the goblet of glee.
Pass me a ribbon that sails to joy ever so endlessly.
Allow me the taste of innocence.
Allow me a cup of peace
And a candle that burns up everything dross
But be careful not to burn me.

Living the Life

Living the life I lead is fun;
Sparkling, bubbly and more.
I can soar to the clouds and stars if I want,
Or I can wrestle my dogs on the Floor.

Peeping around every corner,
Their eyes glistening with glee
Hiding from me but not very far,
One's hiding beneath that tree.

We'll See About That

Aeee shrieked the Siamese cat. Be careful not to step on me.
Cedrick was sleeping under the canopy
Delighting in an afternoon of rest and repose
Eking out a living at everyone's expense.
Fees were being charged by the tax collector
Gee, I shouted, we're taking it up the nose.
He didn't care, it was only his job.
I-yee wailed the cat as the chair pressed his tail.
Jeepers, you do that again and I'll send you to jail.
Keep away from me or I'll scratch you with my claw.
Leeward I swerved; he was a naughty nautical cat.
Meet me at the OK Corral and take that.
Neat of me to say so if I don't mind saying so myself.
Oeee, he scratched me anyway while I wasn't looking.
Peek-a-boo, I see you.
I looked through the back of the chair.
Queen or no queen you're going outside.
Repeat after me – I will not scratch.
See that you learn it before you come back.
Teetering on the brink of day and night
Huey, the cat ran off the porch and took off in flight
Veering to the right, I watched him disappear.
Weeks passed before he came back around here.
Xerox stock took a nosedive that day.
Years passed before it climbed back to stay.
Zebras lost many a stripe over that one.

Free Breakfast Bar

You'll go far
Said the King of Zanzibar.
I can make you a star.
But I was at the Free Breakfast Bar
And didn't want to mar
The Thai Tea
In a jar.

Make a par said the caddy
Driving stuck in tar
Like the guar in ice cream.

I got in my car
Shaped like a jar
Heading far
After a stop with JR
To pick up a cigar.

Taxi Anyone?

One day some chickens came out to play
And they saw a cannon.
They asked their Mommy if they could stay.
And one of them went inside the cannon.

He got blown out.
He had said what's that button for?
He got shot out into the air.
Owwee as he went flying through the air
And landed on his bum-bum over there.

Let's try it again they said.
Except this time he said "Sounds great, it's your turn."
So the other chickens got inside
And they got sent flying for a ride.

Cheek and Beak

Cheek and Beak
Went to sleep
On a Neek
Very sleek

Said Cheek to Beak
Would you take a peek?
No said Beak
To Cheek
I am very meek
And I am bothered
By the beak on my pleak.

What is it you seek?
A mountain peak
Said Beak to Cheek
With a house on top
Of my cheek.
Cheek and Beak
Went to sleep.

Back Seat Passengers

Mom's flowers are dying in the back seat – but who cares.
I've at least had them to enjoy on the trip and feel Mom's
beauty and presence while we drive back to Florida.

At night I'll take them inside the hotel room.
I'll absorb their love and embrace their beauty.
I'll pack them back into the car in the morning for their back
seat ride to Florida.

Puppet Master

I'm not the puppet of your mental state.
I don't surf on the wave of your emotional current.
I don't ride on the street of false desire.
I stand in the center of my being.

Behind the curtain I see stage hands toil
To lift the props into place.
The actors strut and memorize their lines.
The director sips his coffee unaware of anything but the
fragrant moment.

Asleep behind the bench a worker snores but the sound is
drowned out by the magnificent crash of a gong that ends the
early song of a budding star.
You are…all I ever dreamed of, but forgot I was
 dreaming of a time when rhyme was all that mattered.

A broom sweeps the sweeper across the stage
and everything is clean, neat and tidy for the
evening show.

About the Authors & Contributors

Daya Devi-Doolin

Daya Devi-Doolin is a uniquely gifted "thought doctor" and purveyor of wisdom and love. She is the Co-Founder with her husband Chris, and Director of The Doolin Healing Sanctuary & Yoga Studio, in Deltona, FL. She is an internationally known author of metaphysical and self-help books for adults & children. Her inspirational speeches share her secrets for a successful life through an empowering thought system and real life stories. She has assisted hundreds of clients helping them to find health, happiness and success over the past 25 years. Her award winning and best-selling books are: *Super Vita-Minds: How To Stop Saying I Hate You...To Yourself; The Only Way Out Is In: The Secrets of the 14 Realms to Love, Happiness and Success* which is the recipient of the NABE Pinnacle Best Book Achievement Award of 2009 and also *Americans Saving Ourselves Together: How to Thrive in the 21st Century (co-authored) Spring 2010* sold on www.padaran.com, www.amazon.com; **and** www.bn.com. She and her husband Chris form the musical duo *aka Level Seven*. They are songwriters of a variety of styles of music, mainly acoustic adult-contemporary pop music that inspires. Their latest CD and book entitled, *Smile America,* showcases their talent in producing, engineering and arranging the project and writing all the music, lyrics and the book. Daya is a TV/Radio personality offering topics relating to the inherited power of thought and the power behind our *word* which is the cause of manifestation for us. Her weekly show, *The Only Way Out Is In* (based on her best-selling book), airs every Thursday at 2 pm EST, www.blogtalkradio.com/padaran. She is an Ordained Unity Minister, Certified BodyTalk Practitioner, Registered Yoga Alliance Hatha Yoga Instructor (Level 500), Conscious Connected Breath Worker (Rebirther), Certified Reiki Master Teacher, Spiritual Healing Counselor, Matrix Energetics Technician and Motivational Speaker.

"Thoughts area substance and form. They draw unto themselves the likeness of their form." ~Daya Devi-Doolin

Chris Doolin

Chris Doolin is a Recording Engineer and a Microsoft Certified Professional. He graduated from Harvard College with a degree in English and has pursued a lifelong love of music as a songwriter, guitarist, keyboardist and MIDI composer. As a former athlete in basketball and crew, he continues to stay in shape through yoga and biking with his son Joseph on long adventures. He assists Daya with dream seminars, talks on the power of thought, and on occasion with her work as a healer. Daya has two beautiful sons, Tyler and Joseph. Chris and Daya reside with their sons and three pets in Deltona, FL.

Cee Cee Sneed

Cee Cee Sneed is one of our Co-Authors of the Award-Winning book, *Americans Saving Ourselves Together: How to Thrive in the 21st Century.* ~ *"I'm living on the Funny Side of Life and I'm taking as many Americans with me as possible!"* ~ Cee Cee Sneed

Inez Bracy

Her radio show can be heard around the world Tuesdays at 7 PM EST on **www.livingsmartandwell.com**. Be sure to listen and call with your questions or comments at (646) 716-8773. Contact Inez Bracy of the Bracy Group at **Inez@livingsmartandwell.com** with questions, comments or to be a guest on the show. You can watch Inez Wednesday morning on the Fox4 Morning Blend at **www.fox4morningblend.com** sharing tips on Boomers Living Boldly. Inez is one of our Co-authors of the NABE Pinnacle Award-Winning Book Achievement Award for *Americans Saving Ourselves Together: How to Thrive in the 21st Century*. She is also the author of *Rejuvenate Your Life in 21 Days*.

The Contributors of the quote used with Permission from #1 **Best-Selling Authors Chunyi Lin & Gary Rebstock.**

Chunyi Lin – A Certified International Qigong Master, Chunyi Lin is the creator of Spring Forest Qigong, a revolutionary approach to the ancient Chinese practice of health and wellness known as Qigong. In his #1 Best-Selling book, *Born A Healer*, Chunyi offers an inspirational and instructive introduction to Spring Forest Qigong, guiding the reader through the basics of this enhanced healing technique and concluding with the amazing healing stories of some of his students. Since coming to the United States in 1995, he has helped more than 100,000 people learn about the powerful, healing benefits of Spring Forest Qigong.

Gary Rebstock – Co-authored *Born a Healer*. He is a 30-year veteran of broadcast journalism. As a news anchor, reporter and producer, he has received numerous journalism awards from regional Emmys to international film festival honors. Mr. Rebstock is one of only three journalists who have ever interviewed the infamous Burmese warlord Khun Sa, face-to-face. Also known as General Chiang Shi-fu. Khun Sa controls half the world's heroin supply with his ten thousand-man army in the Golden Triangle. ABC News, Nightline and CNN, as well as the local stations have broadcast Mr. Rebstock's reports.

Our Holy Instant With You!

To all our old fans and new fans, our heartfelt thanks for enjoying our music, books and sharing your love and smiles with us along our journey in this Holy Instant!

You can order aka Level Seven CD's & Smile America Books through
http://www.akalevelseven.com
http://www.CDbaby.com/akalevelseven
http://www.padaran.com
http://www.itunes.com

You can preview radio show, books, reviews and suggestions from: http://www.padaran.com/
http://www.blogtalkradio.com/padaran
http://www.freado.com/users/4921/Daya-Devi-Doolin
http://www.twitter.com/dayadevidoolin
http://www.facebook.com/dayadevidoolin
http://www.mauricestarrentertainment.com
http://www.amazon.com/

Here is an excerpt from **The Only Way Out Is In: The Secrets of the 14 Realms to Love, Happiness and Success**, *an award winning book by Daya Devi-Doolin:*

A Solution is Born with the Problem

We all have a level of tolerance for pain, suffering, sorrow, distress and depression. Finally, we may allow ourselves to see the solution. If we really wanted to, the problem could have been solved in an instant because the solution, as I have said, is born with the problem. *A Course in Miracles* (*See Bibliography*) reminds us in the text, that when we remind ourselves there is no problem, then that abolishes it. We have just cancelled out that energy from surviving in our Deeper Mind and allowing It to draw unto us what we really want, Peace.

Stuart Wilde has an exercise in the appendix of his book, *Whispering Winds of Change* published by Hay House. This exercise takes you to a mirror, looking at yourself from inside the mirror. Then you turn your back in the mirror at yourself outside the mirror. There is more detail in his book, but it's a great exercise to find your power and I recommend it to you.

This exercise illustrates that when you take time to go inside yourself and look at yourself objectively, you will always get in touch with the solutions to your problems.

One of Dr. Emmet Fox's stories from a booklet, *The Mental Equivalent,* which comes to mind, is the tale of a prisoner incarcerated in a dungeon for twenty years. He was alone except for the time once a day when the jailer came into his cell to deliver bread and water.

The poor prisoner couldn't stand it any longer and decided to attack the prison guard the next time he brought him some food. He was prepared to defend himself if the jailer tried to kill him.

In preparing, he checked his cell door and discovered it was unlocked! He opened the door, walked past the guards and made his way home.

As Fox pointed out, he could have left at any time if he had known, but he did not. He was a prisoner, not of stone and iron, but of false belief. He thought he was locked in. This was not a true story but an instructional one.

In the Realm of Illusion

In the realm of illusions, we could find ourselves prisoners of resentment, grief, un-forgiveness, sickness, victimization, poverty, indebtedness, sorrow, etc.

All these variations of consciousness represent a lower level of thought that keep us in chains that really do not exist, except in our own minds. Change our thoughts and we are automatically freed, instantaneously.

Take Back Your Power

My suggestion to you is to discontinue allowing the media to give you things to worry about. Place yourself in a protective mode of Light energy every day when and if you decide to listen to the news. Realize that it is not a highly vibrating energy. You do not want that energy stuck in between the molecules and atoms of your lovely structure for any period of time.

Wash yourself of negative thoughts as purposefully as you wash your physical body with fragrant soaps. Clothe yourself in brightly colored light rays that protect you and your children. Block your heart from being sucked into the energy of the media vortex. You will not like the realm of energy it places you in if you allow yourself to be drawn into it.

Don't allow your children (and your thoughts are also your children) to be ensnared by fear and negativity. Teach them to shower themselves with a protective ray of positive energy when they get dressed to go to school, to play games and outings or before watching a TV show. Teach them that they are worthy to be protected both physically and spiritually.

When you enter a room or building, your feet should be "shod in the preparation of peace". Ego cannot recognize you when you are shielded in God's shielding mechanisms. Once you attempt to take off your armor, ego recognizes you and resides, since you are now weak and able to be swayed to its direction.

Celebration

Allow yourself to be dictated to by your Higher Consciousness, your Higher Self, your I am Presence. Allow yourself to receive the answers you are searching for. Find your purpose, your passion. Allow yourself to make your passion work for you and through you. Give of yourself lovingly and freely. Love yourself and find 100,001 ways to celebrate your being-ness here on earth. Find 100,001 ways or 10x that for being in the realm of gratitude!

Instead of believing in your personal lie any longer, believe now that, "I am strong; I am a winner; I am through with being a victim." Repeat those words aloud to yourself with feeling!! At that precise moment, you have stepped over into the Realm of Freedom. All the answers you need to follow through with this new belief will come pouring in rapidly.

In the Realm, in the space of Christ Consciousness, victim mentality is not offered or chosen. The floodgates of truth open up. Awareness of the solution comes as a beam of Light that you could not see before. You were blinded by your own false truth, your own personal lie. Now the door is opened for someone to offer solutions; such as a place for you and your children to live for free; free daycare while you find a job; or free clothes and shoes to choose from in order to go on an interview for a job (or other similar examples that apply in your particular situation).

While I was married ten years to a former husband, I wanted a divorce during the first year. I was ready to leave the day after our wedding day, after one year and then after five years. I stayed because he promised over and over things would be better. They were not.

Blinding White Light

The last period of time I was with him, we had not been intimate for approximately ten months. A day before Thanksgiving, we were invited by friends, who lived in Massachusetts, to come stay with them over the holidays. We lived in Wilmington, Delaware at the time. We didn't find out they had no heat until we arrived. They were renovating an old Boston home in the city. It was freezing cold in our guest bedroom that night. Icicles would have formed on our eyebrows and eyelids if we had stuck our heads from beneath the covers. We had to snuggle to get warm and nature took its course. Moments later, a brilliant flash of white light radiated throughout my womb and mind and I knew my first son had been conceived.

I stayed married until my son was five years old. That's the last time my son saw how abusive his father was to me. The following morning, after his father had tried to strangle me by a chokehold the night before, I sat in the bathroom singing this song softly that I was given, as a gift from Spirit. I was asking if I am ready, Lord. Am I ready to leave, then let it be? Am I ready, Lord, to leave, take my son and manage caring for him on my own? Then, let it be. The words that came to me are below.

AM I Ready Lord? Copyright 1967
Am I Ready Lord? Am I ready Lord?
Am I ready Lord? Am I ready Lord?
Let it Be   If I am ready Lord, If I am ready Lord,
If I am ready Lord, Let It Be! Yes, I am ready Lord.

Yes, I am ready Lord. Yes, I am ready Lord. Let It Be!

I now had a peace, a calmness and a power come into and over me that I had not known since being married.

I got up, got my son and myself ready to leave that morning for good and never looked back. As I walked down the stairs with my son Ty's little hand in mine, I told his father without fear or sadness "I Am leaving!" He could not say anything. He knew that with the power and conviction in my voice, I meant it. He was "blocked" from being violent with me, doing or saying anything to me that would harm me.

We were protected and I knew it. The field of protection felt like an invisible wall three feet wide on all sides of us. There was no fear anymore; there was no sadness and no emptiness within me. Just strength.

Here is an excerpt from **Americans Saving Ourselves Together: How to Thrive in the 21st Century**, edited and co-authored by Daya Devi-Doolin:

Chapter 1
How to Access Your Good

Opening Your Heart

The following article is a summary I wrote of a book on *The Manifestation Process: 10 Steps to the Fulfillment of Your Desires* by John Randolph Price, A Quartus Book Publication. Permission was granted to print this in my last book, *Super Vita-Minds: How To Stop Saying I Hate You...To Yourself,* a Padaran Publication. It is very powerful and I share it here.

    I have found this book very helpful in my life and in sharing it with others through my workshops, seminars and lectures. If you practice or go through the techniques you will find your life heading in the way you wish to see it too. Perhaps you could have a friend do this with you or a loved one who shares your dreams of prosperity, fulfillment and happiness.

    Step 1   Principle of Opening Your Heart. This is based on opening your heart and mind to a spiritual nature. It is tuning into that Presence and Power of God within you. If you don't have this, you will be working with mind power, which offers different results. To get the full impact of the awareness of the Presence, Feel it. Look within and feel it.

Step 2 Principle of Choosing. "Get the thought of what you want as clearly as you can." Make a list of what you want, put it in writing and understand that this is choosing.

By choosing you begin to exercise dominion in all of your life. Spirit will speak to you through intuition, guiding you to choose even greater experiences. All the good that God has for us has already been given to the Reality within us, our Higher Self. We have everything right now, but we have to claim it.

Step 3 Principle of Acceptance. Spirit cannot make the gift available unless you accept it. Only that which you are willing to accept will be yours. All God's gifts to you are first in thought form and when we accept these thought forms a pattern of expression of that thought form is established in consciousness. Once you choose what you want, you accept it mentally and with the fullness of your feeling nature.

Step 4 Principle of Have. When you accept something, you have it even if it is first in the invisible form. When your consciousness accepts that you have accepted it, then it shifts from a sense of need to one of Have. Joel Goldsmith wrote, "By acknowledging that we Have, we shall demonstrate Have."

Step 5 Principle of Visualization. The principle of visualization, through the power of creative visualization, you are in the closest proximity to the activity of God-Mind. This power is called imagination. Through imagination, we have the power to change misfortune into favorable situations, disease into health, unhappiness into joyousness.

This is controlled mental picturing. It's not daydreaming. See yourself having the fulfillment of your desires in the present moment. Always work in the NOW. One way that helps is to look at what you are wearing prior to visualizing. See yourself doing, being, having and enjoying your good as an accomplished fact. Don't see yourself trying to arrange things, like a loan for a car. See yourself as driving your friends, taking trips, etc. Add sound, color and dimension. Watch the people involved with you.

Step 6 Principle of Love. Be sure to love what you are seeing. Generate the warm and beautiful feeling of love and let it radiate through the images in your mind. Love is the power behind the whole thrust of creation. Through the love vibration, you unite the conscious, subconscious and super conscious phases of your mind, and you embody the pattern that represents the fulfillment of your desire.

Step 7 Principle of the Spoken Word. Words that we speak cause a vibration in the universal energy field and the effect of that vibration will return to us in direct accordance with the nature of the word. You let your good come forth and you firmly declare, "It Is Done." The Universe says, "And So It Is."

Step 8 Principle of Surrender. It means we totally and willingly accept the Way, The Truth and the Light of our Higher Consciousness. Let God work out the how, and the details. We must get out of the way of trying to manipulate our good and how it is to come. You will know you have surrendered when you are no longer anxious, concerned, worried and are demonstrating negative energy.

Step 9 Principle of Gratitude. Have a joyful heart filled with praise and thanksgiving, an overwhelming sense and feeling of gratitude because you know that your problems are solved and your needs are met. The secret - be grateful while your good is still invisible! There must be a deep feeling of gratitude in your heart. Gratitude releases a dynamic current of spiritual energy to go before you to exert a mighty influence in your world. It eliminates the negative patterns in the subconscious caused by ingratitude.

Step 10 Principle of Action. Move into action. God's law works through you. Do whatever it is that intuition guides you to do, now! Always listen to that inner feeling for guidance. God can and does meet our needs. We have to act faithful, be faithful and work as if we have what we desire.

Move from fear, doubt and worry. Clean the house, office, car, yard, etc. like it has never been cleaned before, or complete a project you've been putting off. Ask the Holy Spirit what you should do next. Listen as you are being still and then act. Your actions will eliminate your fears. Follow each lead and direction God gives you.

Here is an excerpt from the online book **Easy Steps For Living a Life Free of Fear** by Daya Devi-Doolin:

How to Overcome Depression

Knowing that we are depressed is one of the keys to overcoming depression. Knowing that everything we do involves choice. Everything is choice. Every decision we make, we choose to make it. We decide what we think and we decide what we think is best for us. We can choose again if the result doesn't feel good or feel right. Thoughts are things and there are no thoughts that are neutral, meaning there are no thoughts that have no effect upon your world. Every thought we have has an effect on us because of its power, energy and vibration. No word we put forth from our mouth returns to us void.

Another key or step is **forgiveness**. Forgiveness is the key that parts the way of the Red Sea of your life. You can forgive yourself by saying **"I forgive myself for what I thought I have done. I was mistaken. I apologize to myself. I love myself."**

Forgive another by saying, "I forgive you for what I thought you have done to me. I was mistaken. I apologize to you. I release you to your good. I no longer choose to hold you in my mental prison as responsible." If need to, you can forgive yourself or that person or persons 70 x 7 days until you no longer feel uncomfortable, irritated or depressed.

Another step you might decide or choose is to surrender the struggle, the pain, the anguish, the illness, the hopelessness, the unforgiving nature, and the depression and not claim it as yours anymore. We can stop any thought of ours because it is ours, not anyone else's. Only we can think our thoughts and we can stop any oppressive thought. If it doesn't make us feel good, we can upgrade our thoughts one level at a time to that which makes us feel better emotionally.

How do I stop thinking I am unworthy of anyone's love, anyone's companionship or forgiveness. I can do it by deciding "I am worthy." So, that is what I say and own now, "I am worthy." That is what I claim as the truth for myself. The energy of the words that come forth from you in saying, "I am worthy" puts forth the command to the Universe that you desire something better of life. You will be attracting those aspects of life that prove to you, you are worthy of receiving any desire that is best for you. The Universe will agree with anything you say and believe as real. All you need do is trust, receive and accept your new life's energy.

Decide to change one habit a week. If you drink 10 sodas a day, choose to drink maybe 2 a day, or 2 every other day, or 2 once a week until you down to none a day. Soda wears away the enamel of your teeth and irritates the tissue of your colon and intestines. If you are a shopaholic for example, go on your shopping spree. Then return everything you bought that day and get money back for a vacation you've wanted to take. Or use the money to give to a charitable organization that arranges to give clothes to people looking for job interview apparel. Or you could tithe the money saved to an organization that you feel helps your spiritual growth.

Look into changing what you are now eating. See if some of the foods could be depleting your energy. See if caffeine, chocolate, artificial ingredients need to be taken out of your nutritional intake. See if artificial sweeteners could be adding undue stress for your nerves, muscles, etc. If what you are doing is not working, then you must choose to do something different in order to see something different in your life. Claim a new world by claiming, "I have reasons to be happy. I claim happiness and gratitude." The Universe again, will prove to you that you correct.

And lastly, be grateful. Be grateful where you are in your consciousness now because it is prompting you to know you are in a place that does not make you feel happy. I was homeless at one time and I would not be where I am today if it were not for my being grateful for everything, friends, churches, books, who I was, what desires were placed in my heart, my health, etc. Each level of gratitude I embraced, the Universe doubled it, and gave me back more to be grateful for so now my cup "runneth" over.

Tips:
1. Believe and trust in yourself.
2. Surrender old thought patterns and accept new healthy ones to Christ, God, The Lord, Universal Mind or Infinite Mind.
3. Forgive yourself first and others next.
4. Remember thoughts are not neutral they are things!

How to Get What I Want and Not What I Don't Want!

You will learn to focus on what you want and not what you don't want in your life!

We begin by knowing that we must realize what we focus our energy on is what manifests for us. What we focus on with fear, our subconscious mind matches that fear vibration for us because we have put our energy, feeling, belief and intention behind it and subconscious mind desires only to focus on manifesting that "thing" we are engaged in thinking upon so strongly.

If we focus on what we do want and dismiss what we do not want, subconscious mind focuses on matching that thought vibration (frequency) with the same amount of dedication and energy to bring to us that which we believe is possible. Obama is a great example of what I'm speaking about. He didn't allow anyone to make him think in any way accept fulfilling his destiny, his goal, his plan. Subconscious mind answered him back with the energy of proving to him that he was right about being the President of the United States. If you want to be disgraced, then you must do something disgraceful in order to render that manifestation to yourself through the help of our genie, our subconscious mind. It does not judge your thoughts as good or bad, or unworthy. It honors back to us in matching vibration, that which we believe strongly about whether erroneous or not.

If you want clients for examples or customers, you are telling your subconscious mind you don't believe you have customers or clients so you get more of lack of clients and customers because that is what you are focusing your thought and belief in. When you are grateful for customers and clients that you have, your subconscious mind will begin to work things out for you to confirm your belief in customers and clients and their increase because you have begun to be grateful for things unseen first.

If you are in pain, go the next level of consciousness and start believing all pain has been de-crystallized, dissolved, that the cause has been lifted from your conscious mind and subconscious mind will verify that for you through your belief. You must believe, have faith in and get in the frame of mind by choice and you will receive a new perspective.

If you are out of work, then being in work is what you might want to start holding as the truth for yourself. Telling everyone you are out of work, compounds the belief that you are and subconscious mind will work with you to continue making that a truth for you, even though you say you want to work. Your vibrations are strongly one of being out of work, staying out of work so long as you continue voicing that "truth" which is an untruth. As soon as you begin saying I am in the process of getting a job, then around the corner is a friend of a friend who is hiring your particular qualifications and you find if you had only had belief in the other direction, you might have been working sooner.

Statements like these can help you, "My vision of a trim and fit body is now in the process of becoming a reality; My Health is better than ever; I am succeeding in areas of my life where I never succeeded before; I am on "autopilot"; my body is tireless, filled with energy and power. I am a dynamo, my friends look at me in awe as I power through every day with unstoppable confidence and a passion filled drive to succeed at everything I do! I am in the process of putting into the bank, hundreds of thousands of dollars through all my avenues of abundant God sources of income. I love seeing myself grow spiritually, emotionally and financially. I see all my dreams and goals popping up in rapid manifestation for me like, in days!" Don't push your dreams away from you with doubt, negativity, disbelief and ungratefulness. Accept them!

Padaran Publications
1794 N. Acadian Drive   Deltona, FL 32725
(386) 532-5308
Email: padaran@padaran.com
Web: www.padaran.com   www.akalevelseven.com
PayPal   cdoolin1@earthlink.net

Qty	Description	Unit Price	Total Due
	Smile America CD	$13.99	
	Smile America Book	$12.99	
	The Only Way Out Is In: The Secrets of the 14 Realms to Love, Happiness and Success!	$19.95	
	Americans Saving Ourselves Together: How to Thrive in the 21st Century	$14.95	
	Super Vita-Minds: How to Stop Saying I Hate You...To Yourself	$21.95	
	Returning to The Source	$10.00	
	Hidden Manna: How You Can Interpret Your Dreams	$10.00	
	Dabney's Handbook On A Course In Miracles	$12.95	
	Subtotal		
	Tax where applicable		
	Total		

www.ingramcontent.com/pod-product-compliance
Lightning Source LLC
Chambersburg PA
CBHW070643050426